My name is

_ _ _ _

and I am a
<u>Cumberbitch</u>

HarperCollins*Publishers*
1 London Bridge Street
London SE1 9GF

www.harpercollins.co.uk

First published by HarperCollins*Publishers* 2015

10 9 8 7 6 5 4 3 2 1

Text © Emily Barrett 2015
Illustrations © Alexei Penfold 2015

Emily Barrett asserts the moral right to be identified as the author of this work

A catalogue record of this book is available from the British Library

HB ISBN   978-0-00-814933-8
EB ISBN   978-0-00-814934-5

Printed and bound in the United States of America by RR Donnelley.

The author of this work has made every effort to ensure that the information contained in this book is as accurate and up-to-date as possible at the time of publication. The author and publishers cannot be held responsible for any errors and omissions that may be found in the text.

Find out more about HarperCollins and the environment at
www.harpercollins.co.uk/green

My name is

_ _ _ _ _

and I am a
Cumberbitch

You have a Ben-addiction. This book can help*

HarperCollins*Publishers*

*But probably won't. We're really sorry about that.

Cum·ber·bitch

(kʌmbəbitʃ)

**Variations: Cumbercookies; Cumberologists;
Cumberbabes; Cumbercollective**

♥ Someone afflicted with an appreciation of
the actor Benedict Cumberbatch and his
many wonders (artistic talent, chiselled
cheekbones, twinkling eyes, etc.) to such
an extent that any task not involving him
becomes laborious

*e.g. I physically cannot leave my house today
because I am a Cumberbitch, and Sherlock
series 1–3 is playing back-to-back on TV*

♥ A savvy and sensible person

*e.g. S/he clearly knows a thing or two;
s/he's a Cumberbitch*

~~For Benedict. In whom we trust.~~

For the poor, unsuspecting souls who've yet to lay eyes on the subject of this book, and are therefore unaware of what lies in store for them once they do.

SORRY FOR BEING SO BEAUTIFUL

It's actually not okay, Benedict.

Well, hello there, fellow Cumberlover

1976 will go down in history for many a reason. It was the year Steve Jobs formed Apple Computers, Inc. It was the year someone tried to kill Bob Marley. The UK's 'Save Your Kisses for Me' unsurprisingly won top gong at the Eurovision Song Contest and somewhere in Canada the Olympics happened.

But most importantly, it was the year Benedict Cumberbatch was born – on 19 July, in a rather posh part of London, to parents Timothy and Wanda (better known as Mr and Mrs Holmes in series three of *Sherlock*). Ever since that fateful Monday, we, the common populace, have been blessed with his award-winning films, cracking TV shows, GIFs of his funniest facial expressions and memes of his photobombing prowess. In short, his contribution to modern-day life has been wonderful ...

With the sweet comes the sour

Weekends lost to YouTubing interview clips and compilations of his funniest sound bites. Days fallen prey to box sets and feeling unsatisfied with people who have fewer than six syllables in their name. Hours wasted fantasising about accidentally bumping into him with a skinny cappuccino and what would inevitably happen next. The emotional hangover of what that would do to Mrs Cumberbatch if she ever found out – followed by not feeling guilty at all and hence having to recognise that you're a bad person because of it. It's all right. We've all been there.

Some day you might want to use such productivity and emotional investment elsewhere. School, work, family, travel – things a Ben-addiction can get in the way of. If you've reached this point then what good timing! You are in the right place! Have a quick google to ascertain what BC's favourite drink is, then make one, settle down into an armchair of your choice and begin.

First, we'll run a quick diagnostic check to see if you're in need of our services. Don't panic, it's nothing strenuous, just a quick quiz so we can get a reading on our Cumberometer. If after this it seems you're in need of some rehab, we'll run you through our five simple dis-Batch-ing methods. We can't guarantee anything, but we're sure we'll have you back to life BC (Before Cumberbatch) in no time.

*Some may argue that it's counterproductive to quote from Mr C, but we can't help it that he's a notable source of wisdom in the world today.

'The further you get away from yourself, the more challenging it is. Not to be in your comfort zone is great fun.'

– Benedict Cumberbatch*

So you think you're a Cumberbitch?

♥

So you're definitely a Cumberbitch

♥

So you're done with being a Cumberbitch!

♥

So you think you're a Cumberbitch?

Part 1:
Diagnosis

You've watched every episode of _Sherlock_ twice and you've set up an alert on your phone for relevant Benedict BuzzFeed articles.

But that doesn't necessarily spell trouble; _Sherlock_ is a highly rated, award-winning show after all, and setting up internet alerts demonstrates efficiency and a desire to stay on trend (one hopes ...).

Therefore, to determine where you are on the fan spectrum, we've devised a handy questionnaire for you to complete. Now you can find out once and for all whether you're simply a Cumberbatch admirer, or if you've trespassed into C-word territory.

YOU'VE GOT THIS, GUYS

The Cumberbatch Quiz

Do You

1. Know the name of Mrs Benedict Cumberbatch?

2. Know which film he starred in as Julian Assange?

3. Know which recently reburied King of England he's distantly related to?

4. Know how he formally announced his engagement?

5. Know how he says the word 'penguin'?

6. Know what he was wearing on his lower half (behave) when he collected his 2014 UK National Television Award?

7. Know what his natural hair colour is?

8. Know which of the Marvel Comics characters he's playing?

9. Understand what heterochromia iridis of the eyes means (because he has it)?

10. Now find dragons strangely attractive?

Can You ...

1. Name the 2007 film he starred in as Paul Marshall?

2. Guess his middle names?

3. Recall which British university he received his Bachelor of Arts degree from?

4. Name the musical instrument he had to learn to play for *Sherlock*?

5. Complete the title of this film he features in: *Penguins of _ _ _ _ _ _ _ _ _ _*?

6. Name the famous British boarding school he went to from age 13 to 18?

7. Name the film he starred in alongside Gary Oldman, Colin Firth and Tom Hardy?

8. Describe what he did on his gap year in India?

9. Semi-accurately draw his mouth?

10. Complete this well-known phrase: 'Benedict Cumberbatch is the thinking woman's _ _ _ _ _ _ _'?

Have You ...

1. Seen the 2004 Stephen Hawking drama he starred in?

2. Made/liked/shared a meme of his photobombing-Bono spectacular at the 2014 Oscars?

3. Listened to him read *My Dear Bessie*?

4. Googled Benedict Cumberbatch GIFs?

5. Enjoyed the way he drinks using a straw?

6. Listened to Icelandic band Sigur Rós because you read somewhere that he likes them?

7. Rued the day that the Khan shower scene was cut from *Star Trek Into Darkness*?

8. Considered or actually visited Hampstead Heath – his jogging ground – in the hope of seeing him flit by?

9. Watched the YouTube video of his many celebrity impressions?

10. Ever run your fingers absentmindedly over a photo of his face because you're subconsciously positive you should be able to feel his cheekbones through it?

Would You ...

1. Rather watch:

a) *The Other Boleyn Girl* (historical drama including Benedict for measly minutes before he's killed off)?

b) *War Horse* (Spielberg special of the Michael Morpurgo book of the same name, which features Benedict on a horse for a portion of it)?

c) *The Imitation Game* (heartbreaking film based on real events, with Benedict playing the lead – mathematician Alan Turing)?

2. Go to a première he's attending:

a) Just before the celebs arrive, in the hope of spotting him from the back?

b) Five to six hours beforehand and try to push your way to the front for his autograph?

c) The night before, where you camp out on the red carpet and threaten to chain yourself to the railings should they try to remove you before you've shaken Benedict's hand and shamelessly asked for a selfie?

3. Rate him above the following:

a) A cup of tea?

b) A cup of tea at the Palace?

c) A cup of tea at the Palace with Tom Hiddleston?

4. Rather be which of his following co-stars:

a) Louise Brealey in *Sherlock?*

b) Keira Knightley in *The Imitation Game?*

c) Adelaide Clemens in *Parade's End?*

5. Go to which of the following lengths to meet him:

a) Stand outside the stage door after a production he's in has finished?

b) Find out where he's filming and hang around at the location?

c) Up sticks and move next door to him so you can pop round continuously under the good old 'cup of sugar' pretence?

True or False?

1. He first went to boarding school aged 13.

2. He recorded the voice of Smaug the Dragon for *The Hobbit* lying on his belly.

3. He was abducted in South Africa in 2005 and held overnight at gunpoint.

4. The teenage internet sensation who looks like him is his third cousin.

5. After Benedict photobombed his red-carpet picture, Bono sent him a signed copy of the said item.

6. A play called *Benedict Cumberbatch Must Die* was performed in New Zealand in 2014.

7. He's an ambassador for The Prince's Trust.

8. His inability to say the word 'penguin' stemmed from an attack by the animal he received on a trip to Finland.

9. He officiated his friends' same-sex wedding.

10. He looks great in glasses.

Answers

Do You ...   1 point for every correct answer

1. Sophie Hunter, **2.** *The Fifth Estate*, **3.** Richard III,
4. In the Forthcoming Marriages section of *The Times*
newspaper, **5.** 'Pengling', **6.** Swimming trunks, **7.** Auburn,
8. Dr Strange, **9.** When the irises of your eyes contain
different colours, **10.** Yes.

Can You ...   1 point for every correct answer

1. *Atonement*, **2.** Timothy Carlton, **3.** Manchester, **4.** Violin,
5. *Madagascar*, **6.** Harrow, **7.** *Tinker Tailor Soldier Spy*
8. Volunteered as an English teacher at a Tibetan monastery,
9. Yes, **10.** Crumpet.

Have You ...

Yes answer – 1 point,
No answer – 0 point

Would You ...

'a' answer – 1 point,
'b' answer – 2 points,
'c' answer – 3 points

True or False?

1 point for every correct answer

1. F (he was eight), **2.** T (the clips of him wriggling around are oddly fantastic), **3.** T (very brave, Benedict), **4.** F, **5.** F (but we wish this were true), **6.** T (it's actually a love letter to Ben; we're pretty sure they don't really want him to die), **7.** T, **8.** F (does Finland even have wandering penguins?), **9.** T, **10.** Too bloody right it's true.

Cumber-who?

If you scored 1–14

Being a Cumberbitch is debilitating, but knowing so little about Benedict is equally upsetting for the soul. Perhaps spend some time researching him on popular entertainment websites and then stare at the perfect arches of his eyebrows for a few minutes. The likely outcome will be that you will need this book afterwards.

Cumber-batched

If you scored 15–35

You're heading towards Cumber-crisis, but you're all right for now, and we're secretly quite proud of you for knowing so much about our subject matter. It may be worth checking out **Part 2: Cure** so that you can use the steps as a preventative measure.

Cumberbitch

If you scored 35+

Please take a seat. This might be a little tricky to hear, but we're pretty sure it won't come as a surprise. You're there, in the inner circle, the parameters of peril: the Big C. But it's not a problem! That's exactly what **Part 2** is for. Read on and soon you will be revelling in your return to boring Benedict-less life

'Looking for happiness is a sure way to sadness, I think. You have to take each moment as it comes.'

– Benedict Cumberbatch

So you're definitely a Cumberbitch

Part 2:
Cure

It's understandable. Look at those cheekbones – they could chisel mountains into ice sculptures! There are more GIFs dedicated to them than there are to cats being cute. They even have their own Facebook page, for Pete's sake.

The first thing to remember is, YOU ARE NOT ALONE. While being a Cumberbitch is still considered taboo in some very distant, far-flung corners of the world that we're not too sure exist, this is a phenomenally widespread affliction, affecting whole clusters of society.

The good news is, you've successfully overcome the first hurdle – you've admitted you have a problem and that is the first step to recovery. Well done you! Pat on the back.

And, as with all dependencies, there is a way out. May we present to you:

The Five-Point Plan to Dis-Batch Your Ben-Addiction

Here's how you can put Benedict back in his box . . .

#1
RECOGNISE
THE
DANGER
ZONES

Don't put yourself in the way of turmoil. Just as after a break-up you'd delete your ex from social media and tactically avoid any awkward social situations, so too must you remove yourself from anything that will remind you of Benedict. Here's our handy checklist:

❤ The Isle of Wight

The scene of his wedding. You'll be blubbing at the thought of his morning suit and softly spoken vows before you're off the ferry. (Apologies to the Isle of Wight tourist board.)

❤ Tumblr

Far too many shrines of him talking in slow-mo. It's enough to make anyone dizzy.

❤ World Wide Web

Just in general. It's a dangerous place to be for Cumberbitches. Every goddamn day searches reveal that he's done a new photoshoot or another humanitarian act of kindness.

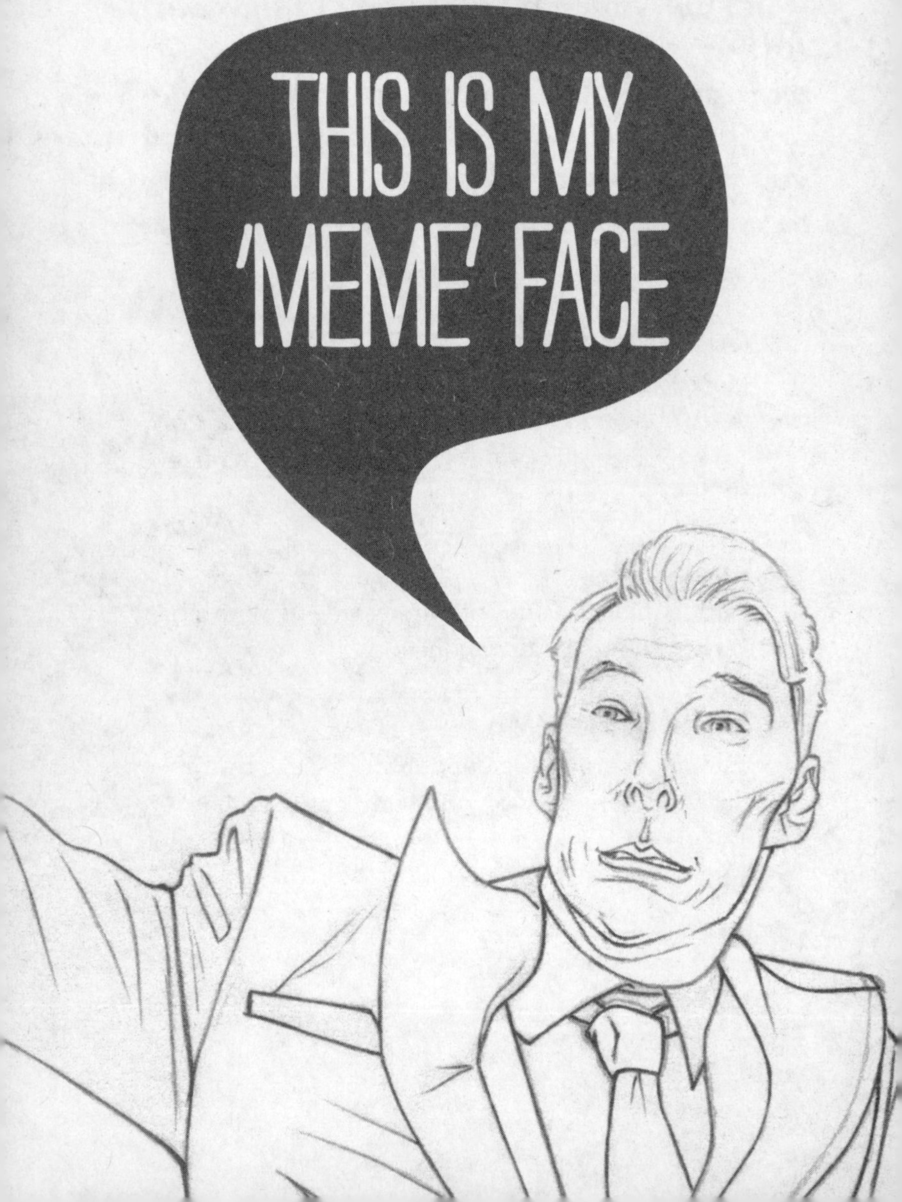
THIS IS MY 'MEME' FACE

❤ Buses and subways

Too many film posters to be safe, unfortunately. While this might be tricky at first, the silver lining is that you'll increase the amount you walk – not only good exercise, but environmentally friendly, too. (Or you could end up driving more, which does neither of those things.)

❤ Magazines and television commercial breaks

Think of all the books you'll read instead! We'd recommend *War Horse*, *Alan Turing: The Enigma* and *The Hobbit*, among others.

❤ The Chelsea Flower Show

An expensive show for posh gardeners in London, which Benedict frequents with his mother. Sucks if you're a keen English horticulturalist, but otherwise this will probably be one of the easier danger zones to steer clear of.

❤ Photobombing

Flashbacks of *that* Bono picture may occur. Don't do it to yourself.

'Enjoy the journey of life and not just the endgame.'

– Benedict Cumberbatch

#2
BITE-SIZED
BENEDICT

Don't ask too much of yourself. Cold turkey can be ever so dry and, let's not be melodramatic, being a Cumberbitch won't kill you – you can afford to wean yourself off a piece at a time. Here's a snack selection you can use to reward yourself if you've been good at #1.

💜 **Visit Tennessee Aquarium's otter**

Following the outcome of an online poll, a resident otter at Tennessee Aquarium was named Benny after Mr Cumberbatch.

💜 **Do something good**

He's so darn charitable, so why not stick up for LGBT rights or feature in fundraising videos to help you feel closer to him? (The secondary benefit is that you will actually be a better person – yay!)

💜 **Hunt down the chocolate statue**

A UK TV channel asked online voters to name the best-looking television drama actor. Benedict won, of course, so they made a life-size chocolate model of the man (as you do). *Literally* bite-sized.

💜 **Watch *Starter for 10***

He's bloody brilliant in it, naturally, and will make you fancy stereotypical nerds forever after, even though he doesn't have a huge part and his slick comb-over leaves a little to be desired.

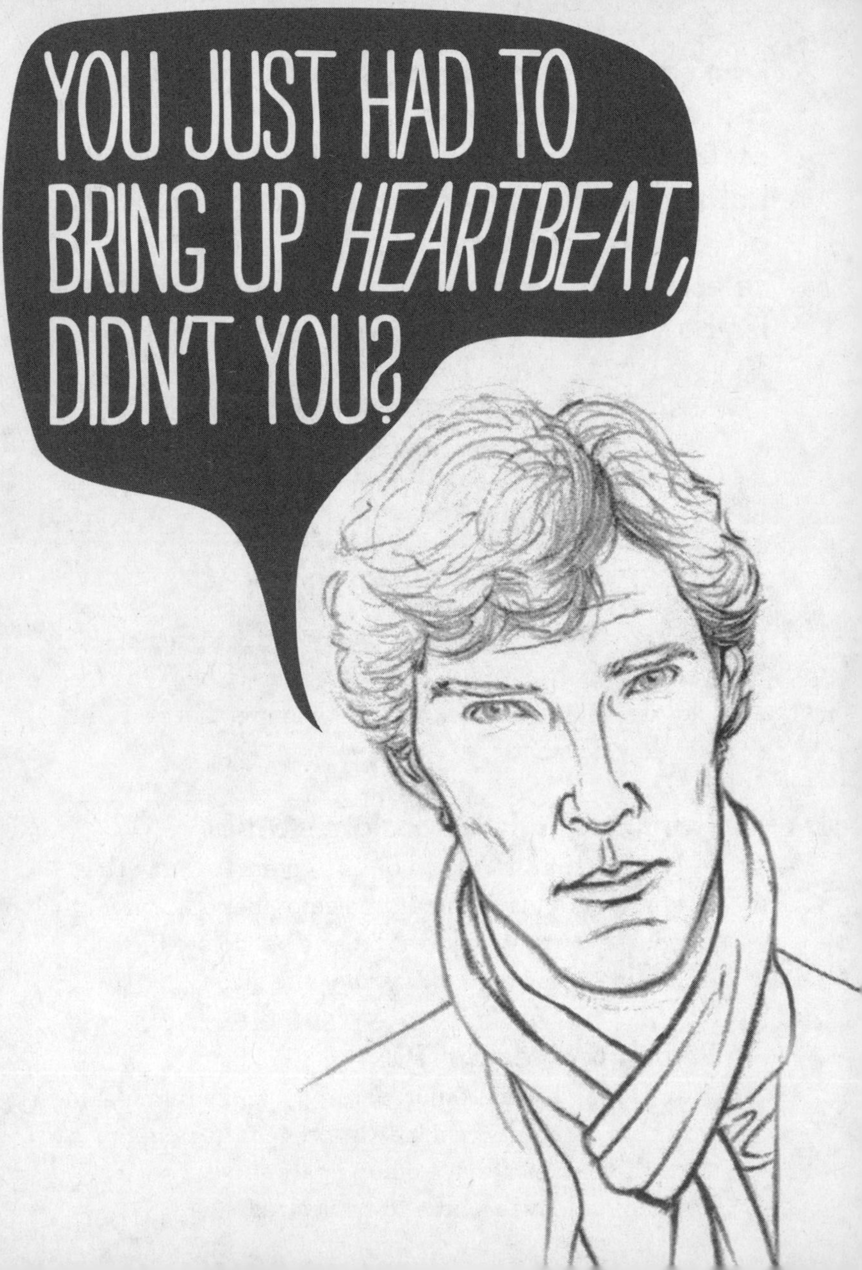
YOU JUST HAD TO BRING UP *HEARTBEAT*, DIDN'T YOU?

♥ Watch *Heartbeat* circa 11 April 2004

A show popular with folk of a certain age, following the lives of 1960s policemen somewhere in the English countryside. Benedict was just starting out, so his powers of attraction will be correspondingly weakened. That's how it works, right?

♥ Take a trip to Madame Tussauds in London

You can get your photo taken with Benedict's waxwork doppelgänger (making you much less likely to stalk the real thing – an arrestable offence. Result!).

♥ Listen to the radio

He's constantly narrating and reading radio parts nowadays, so plenty of opportunities to get your fix without having to face the cheekbones.

♥ Read the news

Remember when he got papped with his hood up holding an A4 piece of paper scribbled with, 'Go photograph Egypt and show the world something important'? Think how happy it would make Ben to know that you're a well-rounded individual, and if his happiness is your happiness . . .

'We all want
to escape our
circumstances,
don't we?'

– Benedict Cumberbatch

#3 NAME ASSOCIATION

Your dad's great. So is your grandma. But they don't produce the same wistful, warm fuzziness in you that Mr Cumberbatch does. After all, can they pull off a suit as well as he can? Probably not.

So here's the trick. Even after identifying your danger zones, you're going to have moments where you come across him unexpectedly. Movie execs will insist on casting him in big-budget productions, after all, and then selfishly advertise them on public transport. Unless you live in the foothills of Mount Tibidabo and can entertain yourself without a television or the internet, you're going to have to face up to those eyes, that mouth, the jawline of legend at some point or other.

But if you can successfully associate a family member with any of his assets, then when they crop up in magazines or on the telly, the edge of your attraction will most certainly be removed. This will inevitably take some time to perfect, but the upside is that you will have to stare at BC's face a lot before you get it right.

☛ Really home in on his chin, while picturing your next-door neighbour

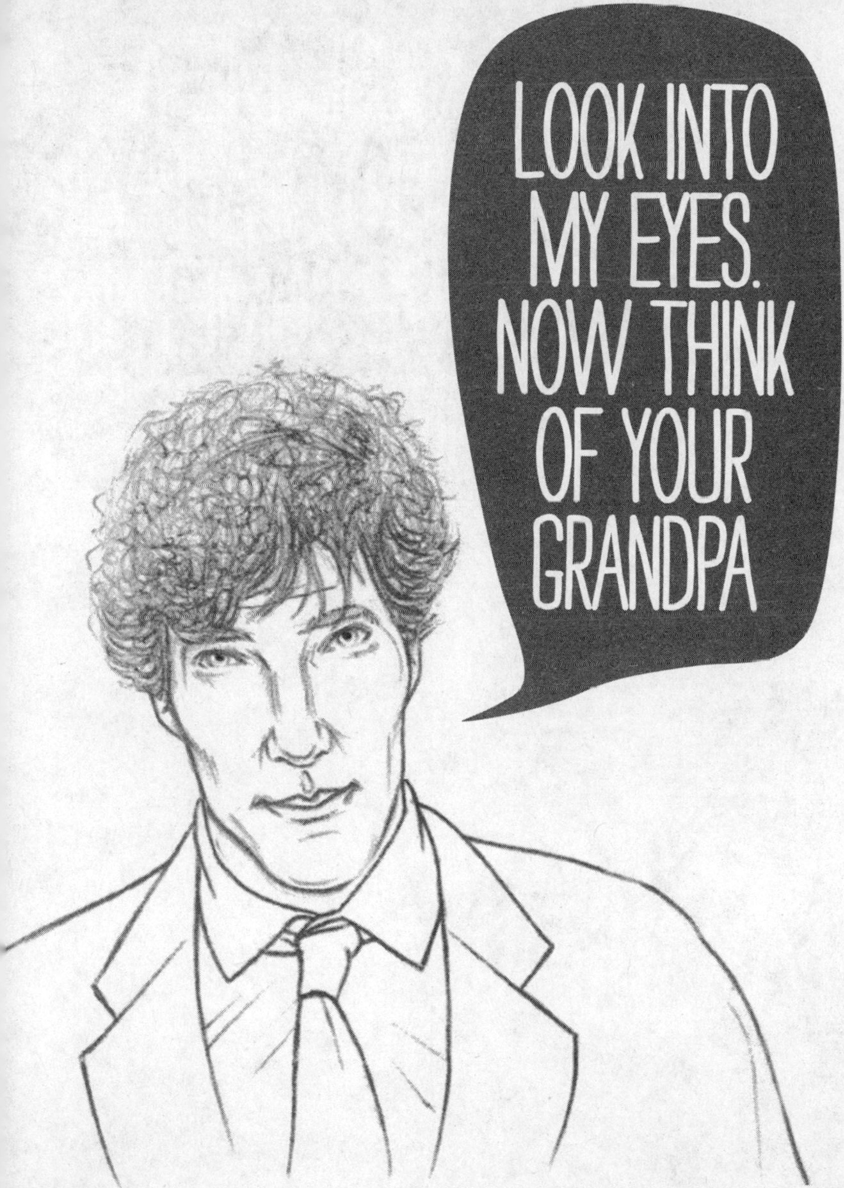
LOOK INTO MY EYES. NOW THINK OF YOUR GRANDPA

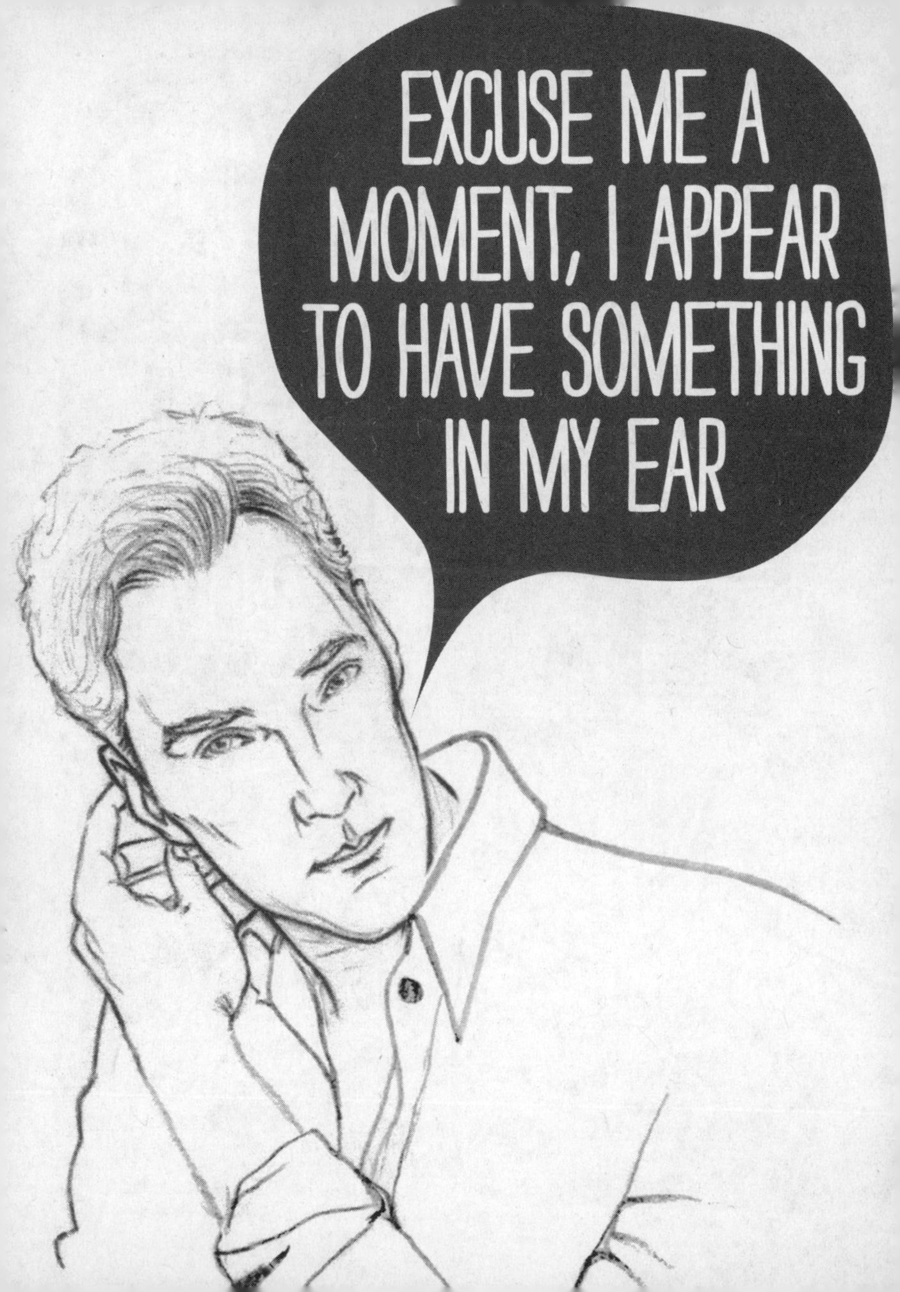
EXCUSE ME A MOMENT, I APPEAR TO HAVE SOMETHING IN MY EAR

See that Adam's apple? Your dad has one, too.

'People should take time to notice, enjoy and help each other.'

– Benedict Cumberbatch

☞ Focus on his hand. Now blur your vision and pretend it's your mum's

Take note of the dimples, and really picture your grandma

'Pull the hair on my head the wrong way and I would be on my knees, begging for mercy. I have very sensitive follicles.'

– Benedict Cumberbatch

#4
A BENEDICT BY ANY OTHER NAME

Benedict Arnold, ladies & gentlemen ☝

The second part to this name association trick is to dilute the name of Benedict. His original brand is, of course, a large part of his appeal, so if we view BC as just another one of the masses it will be much easier to halt the idolatry. Here are some other notable Benedicts to help us do just that.

❤ Benedict Arnold

The simplicity of the surname leaves a lot to be desired, but Benedict Arnold was a sneaky defecting general in the American Revolutionary War. Pretty sexy.

❤ Ben (& Jerry's)

Now here's a Ben worth worshipping. Is Benedict Cumberbatch thick, creamy and living in your freezer? We hope not – but Ben can be!

❤ Eggs Benedict

Two halves of a freshly baked English muffin, topped with just-done poached eggs, crispy bacon and silky hollandaise sauce. Oh, what a breakfast! Oh, what a Benedict!

❤ Benjamin McKenzie

Why not mix it up with a Benjamin? And you remember Benjamin McKenzie, right? Of course you do. He was the 25-cum-16-year-old kid in *The O.C.* who played disadvantaged youth Ryan. Broody, misunderstood and full of Chino angst, who didn't wish they were Marissa (aside from the overdose, the rehab, the dysfunctional family, etc.)?

♥ Pope Benedict XVI

Man of the hour from 2005–2013 for Catholics worldwide. If his gazillion titles don't cast Benedict Cumberbatch into shadow then his papal hat certainly will.

♥ Benedick (you know – from Shakespeare's *Much Ado About Nothing*)

That wily Shakespeare, he knew a good name when he saw one. Horatio, Iago, Lady Falconbridge – and Benedick trumps the lot. Plus, in the guise of Kenneth Branagh back when curtains were the trending hairstyle, he's the epitome of Elizabethan-cum-Nineties fit.

Failing these (frequently) tried and tested techniques, we'd suggest writing to the man himself. First, because he's ever so understanding and wise, and will probably have an answer to your personal dilemma. Second, it's a good way to relieve the angst you're feeling in your Cumberbitch-iness.

We've started it for you here, but feel free to add your own issues. We could even upload it to a petition website – surely we'd be able to get enough signatures from the Cumbercollective to ensure our cause is heard.

Dearest Benedict,

I hope you're well. I hope rehearsals or filming or line learning or whatever else you're doing is also going well, because you're marvellous and your happiness keeps fairies alive.

Conversely, however, I don't hope this. Because I really need to get stuff done, Benedict, and your chiselled features sometimes get in the way of that.

It would therefore be really useful for my future life plans if you could refrain from doing the following:

♥ Being so lovely to your wife

It's really obvious that you're doing it
– we've all seen you in that slow-mo clip
asking her if she's all right on the red
carpet, forever brushing her cheek with
your pouted lips and holding her hand
when you're out walking together.
It doesn't help, either, when you casually
drop into pretty much every interview
how much you value family and how great
you think kids are. I don't want to say
it's selfish, but sometimes, Benedict, I
believe that it is. How can I be expected
to find another half when you're setting
such unattainable standards? My future
happiness is in your hands; either stop
being so publicly wonderful to Sophie,
or leave her and come and find me.

♥ Being so beautiful in photoshoots

That thing you do when you tilt your
face down at an angle but look up so
your forehead furrows and your eyes
twinkle charmingly? Yeah, that's really
unhelpful. Every time you get into a
river in a white unbuttoned shirt, I lose
15 minutes of my day. Finding, gaping
at, emailing and sharing on social media
black-and-white close-ups of your face
looking candidly into the camera has
probably cost me the secret to alchemy,
or some other success-inducing activity.
It would therefore be great if you could

stop doing photoshoots altogether, or at least put a paper bag over your head if you really feel you must.

♥ Being such a skilled artist

I believe this may be the root of the problem, Benedict. Solid drama after solid drama after A-class comedy after solid drama. Chuck us a bone and downgrade to a trashy rom-com every once in a while - if Johnny Depp can do it *cough The Tourist* then why can't you?

♥ Feel free to add your own requests here:

....

....

....

....

....

....

....

....

Yours faithfully

Cumb Erbitch

'Lines are very difficult to learn.'

– Benedict Cumberbatch

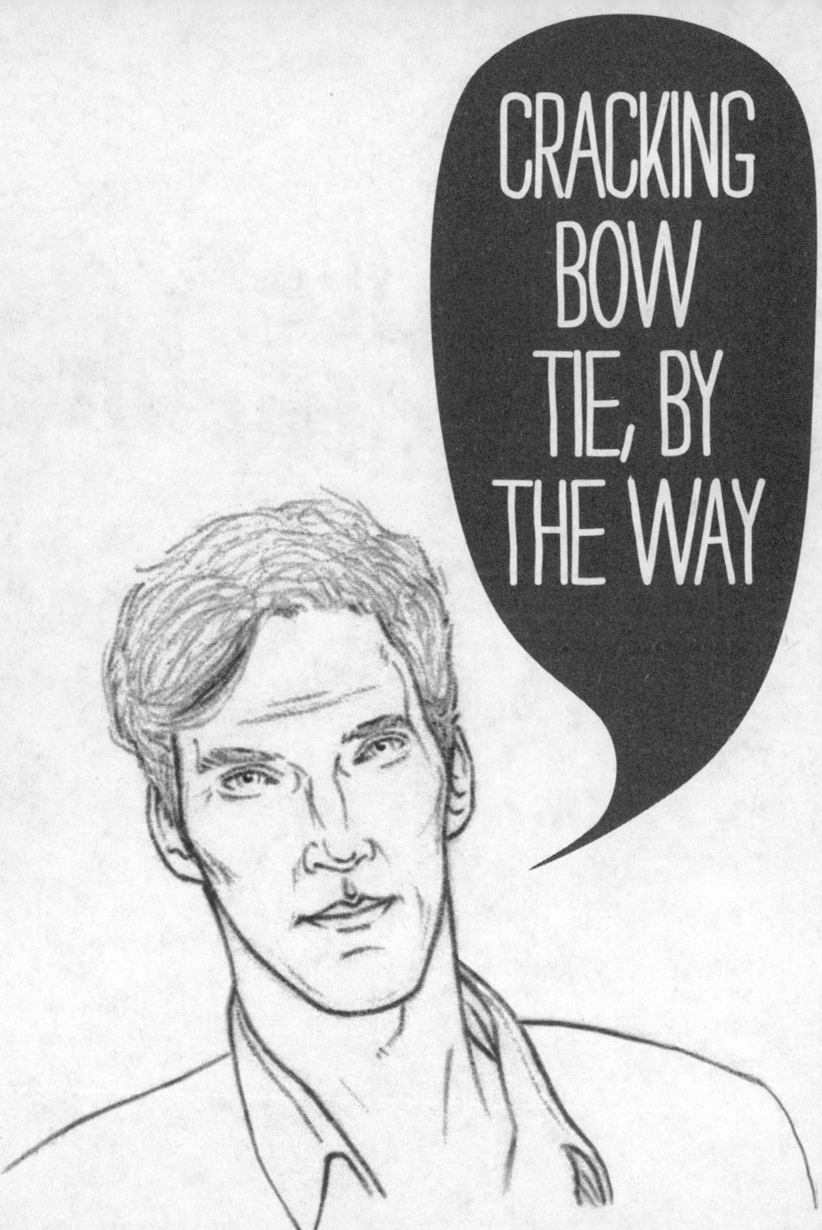
CRACKING BOW TIE, BY THE WAY

CHEERS

So you're done with being a Cumberbitch!

♥

Part 3:
The New You
(maybe)

All done! How do you feel?

Naturally, you feel refreshed and invigorated now that you've escaped the clutches of Cumberbitch-ness, but there's only one way to find out for sure whether you're cured: The Cumberbitch Test – ten questions we've designed to make sure you've ditched that dashing jawline for good.

The Cumberbitch Test

1. What would you rather do with the next ten minutes?

a) Watch the cut Khan shower scene.

b) Anything else.

2. Google images of 'Benedict Cumberbatch eyes'. How do you feel?

a) Ecstatic.

b) Nothing (well, not nothing – I'm still human).

3. Watch an episode of *Sherlock*. Who would you prefer to cuddle out of Sherlock or John?

a) Sherlock.

b) Either. I'm not fussy.

4. What emotion do you feel when you think of Benedict in a tux?

a) So excited I'm about to burst.

b) A tux is just apparel, so of course I don't feel anything.

5. You bump into Benedict Cumberbatch in the street. What do you do?

a) Barely contain myself and stammer so much while requesting a hug and a selfie that I coin a new word: 'helfie'.

b) Remark that it's that actor from the telly and politely stop him so as to tell him he's rather good.

6. You have tickets to see a play that Benedict is starring in, but at the last minute your grandma calls to say she's feeling poorly. What do you do?

a) Nan's tough as nails. TLC can wait until the morning.

b) It's a shame, because theatre tickets are bloody expensive, but I should really spend the night looking after Nan if she's ill.

7. You're messing around on the internet. You are:

a) Checking out Tumblrs/humorous BuzzFeed articles devoted to Benedict.

b) Shopping/social media-ing/working/emailing, etc.

8. What are you daydreaming about?

a) Benedict holding me.

b) World peace.

9. It's dark and you hear a noise outside. You're frightened. Who do you wish was around to protect you?

a) Benedict Cumberbatch.

b) The police/The Rock/a dog/Mum.

10. You're in a bookshop and spot a self-help guide entitled *My Name Is X and I Am a Cumberbitch*. What's your reaction?

a) Think, 'I need it and will thus buy it immediately.'

b) Laugh. Think, 'What a witty little book! I think Sally's a fan of his, perhaps I should buy it for her.'

Outcome

Pine Nut

If you scored 0–3

You're cured! Well done you! (And well done us for doing the curing!) Have fun-loving Chris Pine instead – he's a very gorgeous man.

Cumberbitch

If you scored 4+

Well, this is a bit awkward.

So you're done with being a Cumberbitch – that's great news, we're so happy for you! Go forth, prosper and don't worry about that vague, empty, restless feeling – it will pass.

Hang on a second. What do you mean, 'No'? You mean to say that our super-helpful little guide hasn't cured you of said affliction?!

We can't say we're too surprised. He's a beautiful specimen of man. And (between us) here at dis-Batching headquarters, we're not honestly convinced that being a Cumberbitch is a bad thing anyway. After all, he's smart, charitable, seems to know a thing or two about current affairs and he has a cracking set of cheekbones.

(We should mention here that we're also not particularly qualified to give out rehabilitating advice, so if it *had* worked we would have been immensely impressed with ourselves. Don't look so shocked – what do you think the asterisk on the front cover is for?)

So instead of trying to oust our Ben-addictions, perhaps we should be embracing them instead. After all, when life gives you lemons, one grabs the tequila, so when life gives you a Cumberbatch, you become a Cumberbitch. It seems rather rude not to.

Let us rally together behind the Cumberbatch banner, stick our flag boldly in the ground and declare that we are Cumberbitches and proud to be so.

I
am
Cumberbitch!

...are you?

Acknowledgements

Thanks to Benedict, without whom this book would not have been possible. Thanks for wearing such great glasses. Thanks for being able to swag like Beyoncé. Thanks for partaking in interviews and providing such witty answers. Thanks for wearing open-neck shirts and tuxes with bow ties. Thanks for coiffing your hair and for slicking it back. Thanks for making such fabulous television and film appearances (should we also thank LAMDA here for helping you on your way? Okay then, thanks LAMDA).

We'd thank you for your stage performances as well, but we've never been able to get a ticket. Damn thespians and other Cumberbitches for that.

Thanks for being such good friends with Martin Freeman. That bromance floors us. Thanks for doing posey photoshoots with trees and dogs, but also thanks for pulling funny faces. Thanks for that time at the Oscars in 2015 when you drank out of a hip flask while saying, 'Go away.' That was funny.

We'd thank Timothy and Wanda for your face, but that seems a bit beside the point, although your face is great. Thanks for making fireworks go off around your head and Sixties soul start playing when you come on screen. Thanks for wearing scarves, and flicking the collar on your coat, and having such a reverberating deep voice, and for doing *Starter for 10*, because, you know. Mostly, thanks for being Alan Rickman that time in *The Simpsons*.

Thanks, Benedict. You're a real keeper

'I believe the sense of humour is important.'

– Benedict Cumberbatch